J   Allen, Kathy
BIO
BRADY   Tom Brady

Tom Brady

by Kathy Allen

Consultant: Barry Wilner
AP Football Writer

BEARPORT
PUBLISHING

New York, New York

Credits

Cover and Title Page, © Robert E. Klein/AP Images and David Drapkin/AP Images; 4, © Mike Segar/Reuters; 5, © Tom DiPace/AP Images; 6, © Seth Poppel/Yearbook Library; 7, © Mark Humphrey/AP Images; 8, © Seth Poppel/Yearbook Library; 9, © Junipero Serra High School, San Mateo, California; 10, © Carlos Osorio/AP Images; 11, © Joe Robbins/Getty Images; 12, 13, © John Biever/Icon SMI; 14, © Jim Bourg/Reuters; 15, © Bob Falcetti/Icon SMI; 16, © Kathy Willens/AP Images; 17, © Bob Falcetti/Icon SMI; 18, © David Drapkin/AP Images; 19, © G. Newman Lowrence/AP Images; 20, © Mark Humphrey/AP Images; 21, © Chris Keane/ Icon SMI; 22, © John Biever/Icon SMI.

Publisher: Kenn Goin
Senior Editor: Joyce Tavolacci
Creative Director: Spencer Brinker
Photo Researcher: Arnold Ringstad
Design: Emily Love

Library of Congress Cataloging-in-Publication Data

Allen, Kathy.
  Tom Brady / by Kathy Allen.
      p. cm. — (Football stars up close)
  Includes bibliographical references and index.
  ISBN 978-1-61772-717-7 (library binding) — ISBN 1-61772-717-2 (library binding)
  1. Brady, Tom, 1977—Juvenile literature. 2. Football players—United States—Biography— Juvenile literature. I. Title.
  GV939.B685A55 2013
  796.332092—dc23
  [B]

For more information, write to Bearport Publishing Company, Inc., 45 West 21st Street, Suite 3B, New York, New York 10010. Printed in the United States of America.

10 9 8 7 6 5 4 3 2 1

Contents

Super Start

Quarterback Tom Brady stood in the middle of the field. Confetti rained down all around him. His team, the New England Patriots, had just won the 2002 **Super Bowl**. As fans cheered from the stands, Tom raised his arms in the air and shook his head. He could not believe what he had just done.

Tom walks off the field after leading his team to a Super Bowl win.

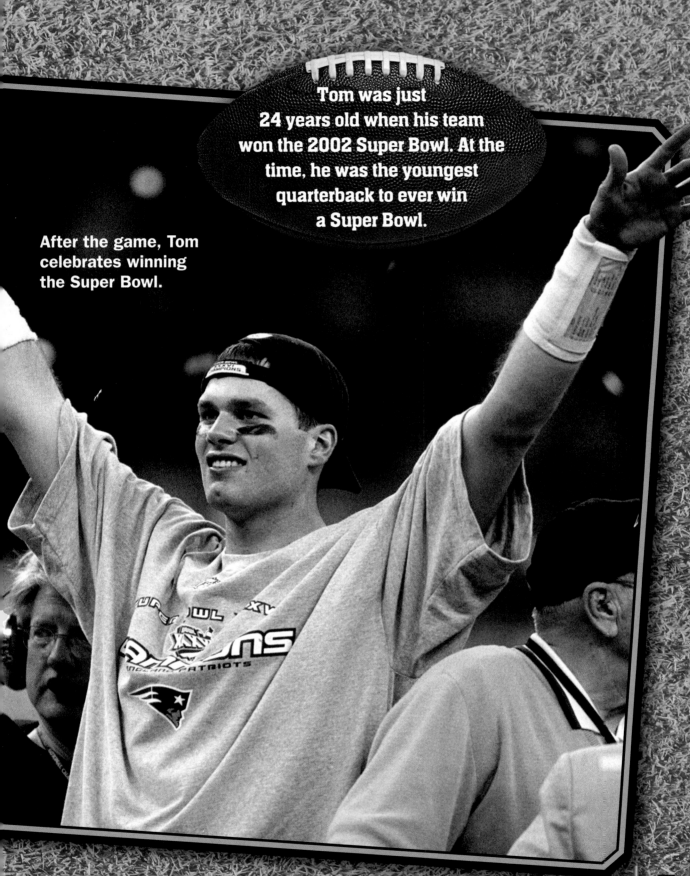

Tom was just 24 years old when his team won the 2002 Super Bowl. At the time, he was the youngest quarterback to ever win a Super Bowl.

After the game, Tom celebrates winning the Super Bowl.

The Little Brady

Tom was born in San Mateo, California, on August 3, 1977. When he was a boy, no one thought he would become a football star. He had three older sisters who were all great **athletes**. Tom was a good baseball player, but he was small and not very fast on his feet. Because of his size, Tom's parents worried he would get hurt if he played football.

Tom's ninth-grade yearbook photo

Tom's sisters, Maureen, Julie, and Nancy, were outstanding soccer and softball players.

Tom with
his parents
in 2012

Better at Baseball

However, Tom really loved football. He finally got a chance to play in ninth grade. He became the team's **starting** quarterback in eleventh grade, but the team won few games. Tom also played on his high school's baseball team. Although Tom was better at baseball, he stuck with his favorite sport, football.

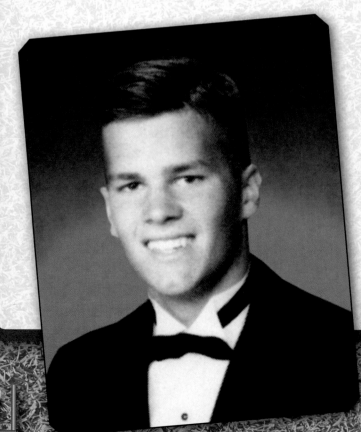

This yearbook photo was taken during Tom's senior year.

Tom throws a pass while warming up for a high school game.

The Montreal Expos baseball team selected Tom as a catcher in 1995, but he decided to focus on football.

Going to Michigan

When it was time for Tom to go to college, he decided to attend the University of Michigan. The Michigan Wolverines had a strong football team. Tom would have to work extra hard to earn playing time. In his first two years at the school, however, he spent most of the games sitting on the bench.

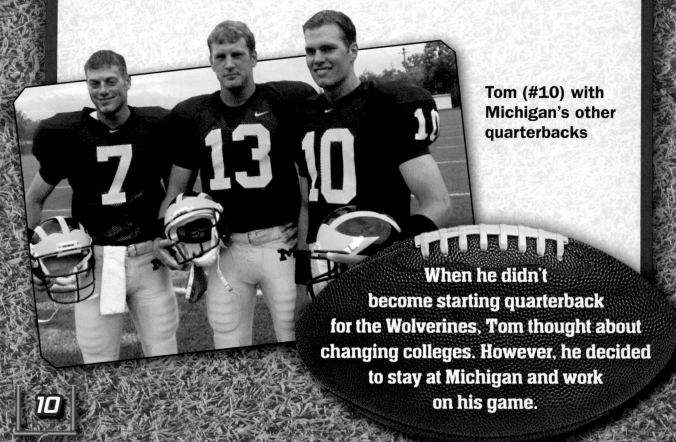

Tom (#10) with Michigan's other quarterbacks

When he didn't become starting quarterback for the Wolverines, Tom thought about changing colleges. However, he decided to stay at Michigan and work on his game.

Tom watches a Wolverine's game from the bench at Michigan.

Finally a Starter

Tom finally became the starting quarterback in his junior year at Michigan. Tom was still not very fast. However, he had learned to sidestep **tacklers**. He also used his strong **passing** arm to help set up his team to score **touchdowns**. In his two years as the starting quarterback, the Wolverines won 20 out of 25 games.

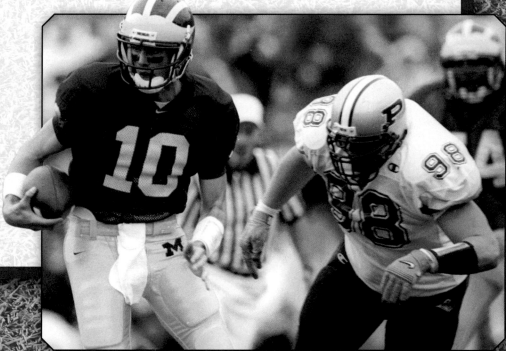

Tom moves to avoid a tackle by a defensive player on the other team.

Tom is about to launch the ball in a 1999 game at Michigan.

Tom impressed his coaches with his playing and leadership skills. At the end of the season, he was named a **team captain**.

Slow Start

Although Tom was a great player at Michigan, many **NFL** teams thought he was too skinny or too slow. The New England Patriots finally chose Tom in the sixth round of the 2000 NFL **draft**. The Patriots already had Drew Bledsoe as their starting quarterback, so Tom spent his first season watching and learning.

Tom (right) talks with Drew Bledsoe in 2001.

When Tom was drafted, the Patriots already had a starting quarterback, Drew Bledsoe (#11).

Tom was picked 199th out of 254 players in the NFL draft. He was frustrated that he wasn't chosen sooner.

Sudden Rise

Early in Tom's second NFL season, Drew Bledsoe was injured. No one was sure if Tom was ready to lead an NFL team, but it was time to find out. Tom started the rest of the Patriots' games that season. His leadership and accurate passing helped the Patriots win 11 out of 16 games. Tom followed that up by leading the team to its first Super Bowl victory!

Tom was named the MVP of the Super Bowl in 2002.

Tom receives the Super Bowl MVP trophy.

Tom prepares to throw a pass as the Patriots' starting quarterback.

More Success

After his Super Bowl victory, Tom Brady became an NFL superstar. Over the next three seasons, his star would continue to rise. The Patriots missed the **playoffs** in 2002 but came back to win both of the next two Super Bowls. Only three other quarterbacks in history have led their teams to three or more Super Bowl wins. Tom did it in only four years!

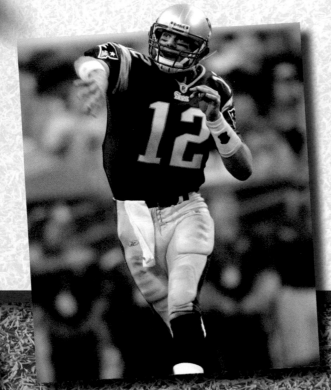

Tom hurls a long pass during the 2004 Super Bowl.

Tom calls out a play during the 2005 Super Bowl.

Tom won his second Super Bowl MVP award playing against the Carolina Panthers in 2004.

Still a Star

Tom has continued to be a great player. In 2007, he set an NFL record with 50 touchdown passes and led the Patriots to the first 16–0 record in NFL history. He won the league MVP award in 2007 and again in 2010. All of Tom's hard work has shown that you don't have to be the biggest or fastest player to be among the best.

Tom embraces his mother before a game in 2012.

Tom had more **passing yards** in 2011 than ever before. He passed for a stunning 5,235 yards (4,787 m).

Tom celebrates after throwing a touchdown pass during the Patriots' perfect 2007 regular season.

Tom's Life and Career

★ **August 3, 1977**   Tom Brady is born in San Mateo, California.

★ **1998–1999**   Tom leads the University of Michigan to 20 wins in 25 games.

★ **2000**   Tom is drafted by the New England Patriots.

★ **2002**   The Patriots win the Super Bowl, and Tom wins his first Super Bowl MVP award.

★ **2004**   The Patriots win the Super Bowl, and Tom wins his second Super Bowl MVP award.

★ **2005**   Tom leads the Patriots to their third Super Bowl win in four seasons.

★ **2007**   Tom throws a record 50 touchdown passes and is named the NFL's MVP.

★ **2010**   Tom is named the NFL's MVP for the second time.

★ **2011**   Tom throws for 5,235 passing yards (4,787 m), a new personal record

★ **2012**   Tom leads the Patriots to the Super Bowl for the fifth time.

Glossary

athletes (ATH-leets)
people who are trained in or are
very good at sports

draft (DRAFT)
an event in which professional
football teams take turns choosing
college athletes to play for them

MVP (EM-VEE-PEE)
letters standing for the most
valuable player, an award given to
the best player in a game or in a
season

NFL (EN-EFF-ELL)
letters standing for the National
Football League, which includes
32 teams

passing (PASS-ing) throwing

passing yards (PASS-ing YARDZ)
the distance that a quarterback
throws the ball, plus the distance
the receiver runs after the catch

playoffs (PLAY-awfs)
games held after the end of
the regular football season that
determine which two teams will
compete in the Super Bowl

quarterback (KWOR-tur-bak)
a football player who leads the
offense, the part of a team that
moves the ball forward

starting (START-ting)
being the coach's first choice to
play in a game

Super Bowl (SOO-pur BOHL)
the final championship game in the
NFL playoffs

tacklers (TAK-lurz)
defensive players who try to knock
whoever has the ball to the ground

team captain (TEEM KAP-tin)
a title given to a player who shows
leadership on a team

touchdowns (TUHCH-*douns*)
scores of six points that are made
when a football player gets the ball
across the other team's goal line

Index

Bibliography

Official Site of the New England Patriots: www.patriots.com

Official Site of the NFL: www.nfl.com

Pierce, Charles P. *Moving the Chains: Tom Brady and the Pursuit of Everything*. New York: Farrar, Straus and Giroux (2006).

Read More

Glaser, Jason. *Tom Brady (Sports Idols)*. New York: PowerKids Press (2008).

Sandler, Michael. *Tom Brady and the New England Patriots: Super Bowl XXXVIII (Super Bowl Superstars)*. New York: Bearport (2008).

Scheff, Matt. *Tom Brady: Football Superstar (Superstar Athletes)*. Mankato, MN: Capstone (2012).

Learn More Online

To learn more about Tom Brady, visit
www.bearportpublishing.com/FootballStarsUpClose